RECEIVE YOUR HEALING NOW!

A PRACTICAL APPROACH TO DIVINE HEALING

RECEIVE YOUR HEALING NOW!

DAVID ADEOLA ADEBOYE

XULON PRESS

Xulon Press
2301 Lucien Way #415
Maitland, FL 32751
407.339.4217
www.xulonpress.com

© 2020 by David Adeola Adeboye

Receive Your Healing Now!

All rights reserved solely by the author. The author guarantees all contents are original and do not infringe upon the legal rights of any other person or work. No part of this book may be reproduced in any form without the permission of the author. The views expressed in this book are not necessarily those of the publisher.

Unless otherwise indicated, Scripture quotations taken from the King James Version (KJV) –*public domain*.

Printed in the United States of America.

ISBN-13: 978-1-6312-9197-5

TABLE OF CONTENTS

DEDICATION vii
ACKNOWLEDGEMENT. ix
INTRODUCTION xi
1. GOD'S WILL FOR YOUR HEALTH 1
2. FAITH: OUR ACCESS KEY! 7
   What Is Faith? 7
   How Does Faith Come? 11
3. THE POWER OF CONFESSION 17
   Positive Confession. 17
   Negative Confession 20
   God Backs What You Say 22
   The Angels Act on What You Say. 23
   Satan Bows at Your Word 23
4. YOU NEED A POINT OF CONTACT 27
5. THE ANOINTING OIL 33
6. THE COMMUNION OF HEALING 39
7. THE HEALING WATER 45
8. THE HEALING MANTLE 49
9. PRAYING FOR DIVINE HEALING. 55
10. SEVEN RULES OF FAITH FOR
    DIVINE HEALING 63
    ONE: Recognize that Sicknesses and Diseases
    Are Oppressions of the Devil. 64

    TWO: Believe the Message.................67
    THREE: Go to Where the Power Is.......... 68
    FOUR: Put Your Faith in God, Not Man...... 69
    FIVE: Accept the Correction of God......... 72
    SIX: Lose Yourself....................... 72
    SEVEN: Use a Point of Contact. 73
11. MAINTAINING DIVINE HEALTH 77
    1. FAITH............................... 78
    2. LOVE 78
    3. FASTING 79
    4. CONFESSING THE SCRIPTURE......... 80
    5. YOUR SERVICE IN GOD'S HOUSE......81
    6. HOLINESS 82
25 HEALING SCRIPTURES...................85
HELPFUL PRAYER POINTS 91

DEDICATION

To my mum, Josephine Boladale Adeboye,
a woman of faith and substance.
Your faith in God and your dedication to His
service has made you a role model for me to follow.
Thanks for believing in me when nobody else could.
You are the best mother ever!

Acknowledgement

This book was born out of the inspiration of the Holy Spirit; however, it went through many stages of production, and I would like to acknowledge with much appreciation all those who played significant roles in making this book a reality. Special thanks to Evon N. Korbieh for typesetting and putting the manuscript together for us to enjoy. What a great blessing you have been around us and our ministry. May the God that we serve in the gospel of our Lord Jesus Christ bless and increase you greatly.

To my friend and co-worker Marcus Thomas, who took time to proofread the book over and over again for accuracy in presentation and to make sure the editing was done properly. Thanks so much for your work to make the book a masterpiece for us to read; may the Lord bless you and your family in Jesus's name.

Also, to all the members and partners of Champions Chapel International in Houston, Texas, and David Adeboye Ministries around the world, I say a big thank-you for supporting and partnering with me to make a difference in the world.

Last, but definitely not least, to my amazingly blessed and awesome wife, Abiose Omolola Adeboye: I can say without a doubt that marrying you is the best thing that ever happened to me, apart from my salvation in Christ Jesus. I really appreciate you for always being there for me and standing with me in life and ministry. I love you sincerely, girl!

Introduction

THE DEVIL IS ALWAYS DEPRIVING PEOPLE of enjoying good health every day, having inflicted a lot of people in this world with the bondage of all manners of sickness and diseases. Sicknesses and diseases are not only from the devil; some came from the way we use our bodies and what we eat. The body of a man is like a machine that works all the time, so it needs rest, maintenance, and good care: and when we don't take these issues to heart, we will have sickness as a result of not resting, not caring for our bodies, and eating the wrong food.

While this book is not to discuss how to care for your body and what kind of food you need to eat, as there are already many good books on those subjects, it is to let everyone know that no matter what caused a sickness or disease in your body, God is still there to heal you of them all.

Some time ago, when a family member was involved in an auto crash, I went to visit her at a very big hospital complex. During my visits to her, I saw all manner of people being afflicted with different kind of sicknesses and diseases, no matter their caliber. I saw both young and old, rich and poor, spending their days in pain and agony and having no way out of these problems. During my visit, I discovered that many people have even become materials for doctors to practice on, simply because of one sickness or the other. I, therefore, was inspired with a strong passion to write this book for everyone to understand the mind of God concerning their health, whether they are healthy or sick, and for the sick people trusting God for their healing and to understand the steps to getting healed. This book gives practical approaches to the subject of divine healing, how to receive it, and how to stay perfectly healthy throughout life.

I so believe that as you take time to read this book, you will never be the same again, and that all the sick people who lay their hands on this book shall be healed in the name of Jesus Christ. Amen!

Receive Your *Healing* Now!

"Beloved, I wish above all things that thou mayest prosper and be in HEALTH, even as thy soul prospereth." 3 John 2

Chapter One
GOD'S WILL FOR YOUR HEALTH

IN EVERY ASPECT OF LIFE, THERE IS THE perfect will of God in His word for His children, so that they may understand His heart about it and live according to it. There is a perfect will of God concerning your health as a child of God. He has decreed certain things concerning you in His word. We will take time to examine the Word of God to discover the passages that show His will concerning our health as His children.

> *"Beloved, I wish above all things that thou mayest prosper and be in HEALTH, even as thy soul prospereth." 3 John 2*

The passage above was written by the apostle John, declaring the mind of God for our lives. This verse makes clear that God wishes for you to prosper and have good health. It is His will that you live in good health. Your vitality is God's priority, and anything contrary to this message is not of God. God is a good God and a loving father who loves His children; therefore, He cannot wish you pain and agony, and cannot have pleasure in your pain because that would be contrary to His word.

The Gospel of John in chapter 3, verse 16 says:

"For God so loved the world that He gave His only begotten Son, that whosoever believeth in Him should not perish, but have everlasting life."

Can a loving God who gave His only begotten Son, for the sake of our sins, give us sicknesses and diseases to afflict us at all? No, the Bible says in Romans 8:32 that:

"He that spared not his own Son, but delivered him up for us all, how shall he not with him also freely give us all things?"

If He can give His Son for us, what else can He refuse to give us? There is absolutely nothing God won't give us to bring enjoyment in all areas of our lives. You will be glad to know that Jesus Himself came not only to take our sins away, but also to HEAL all sicknesses and diseases. Before He came, there was a prophetic proclamation concerning the purpose of His coming that speaks about our healing. Isaiah 53:5 says:

"But he was wounded for our transgressions, he was bruised for our inequities: the chastisement of our peace was upon him; and with his stripes we are healed."

Can you see now that even before He came, He made provisions to deal with sicknesses and diseases so we may not be afflicted with them again? The New Testament established the fulfillment of the above passage in 1 Peter 2:24:

"Who his own self bare our sins in his own body on the tree, that we, being dead to sins, should live unto righteousness: by whose stripes ye were healed."

When Jesus came to this world, He was absolutely against sicknesses and diseases, and He ministered to a lot of people who were sick.

"When the even was come, they brought unto him many that were possessed with devils: and he cast out the spirits with his word, and HEALED all that were SICK: That it might be fulfilled which was spoken by Esaias the prophet, saying, Himself took our infirmities, and bare our sicknesses." Matthew 8:16–17 (emphasis added)

Can you see what he did? He healed all who were sick: He never allowed one sickness to escape His word of healing, and He drove out devils, the root cause of all sicknesses.

So many passages in the Gospels demonstrate how serious Jesus was against sicknesses and how He healed many people. Even when He was sending His apostles out, He also sent them against sicknesses:

> *"And when he had called unto him his twelve disciples, he gave them power against unclean spirits, to cast them out, and to heal all manner of sickness and all manner of disease." Matthew 10:1*

He later commanded the apostles to do the following:

> *"Heal the sick, cleanse the lepers, raise the dead, cast out devils: freely ye have received, freely give." Matthew 10:8*

Jesus showed the apostles examples of healing the sick during His preaching ministry:

> *"And Jesus went about all the cities and villages, teaching in their synagogues, and preaching the gospel of the kingdom, and HEALING every SICKNESS and every*

DISEASE among the people." Matthew 9:35 (emphasis added)

He sent the apostles to heal all MANNER of sickness and disease. Glory be to God that what God was doing was what Jesus Christ came to do, and the same thing He sent the apostles to do, is the same assignment He has handed over to us today to do.

With all these things that have been said, it is pertinent to state clearly that God is committed to give good health only to those who are His. Therefore, if you are not His child, you may not have access to His blessing of divine healing. To get His blessing of divine healing, you must become His child by giving your life to Him. Accept Him as your Lord and your Savior, surrender all of your life to Him, and decide to follow and serve Him. If you do so, He will then be committed to heal you of all your sicknesses and diseases.

Now that we understand the will of God concerning your health, let's discuss how we can be healed from sicknesses and diseases, and how to stay healthy throughout the days of our lives.

"Now faith is the substance of the things hoped for, the evidence of things not seen." Hebrews 11:1

Chapter Two
FAITH: OUR ACCESS KEY!

IF YOU ARE SICK AND YOU WANT TO BE healed, you will need to develop your faith for divine healing. Faith is the major key to getting anything from God; it is the link between your problem and the power of God that will bring the solutions to you. Until you connect to faith, your healing might be impossible, because you need faith to move God to heal you.

WHAT IS FAITH?

Faith can be defined as an expression of confidence in God and His word. Faith is the ability to see what you are praying for as a gift in your hand already. As God Himself said, faith means believing you have something—even when you cannot see the physical proof yet—because God said it is yours. Let us look at the definition of faith from Hebrews 1:1, from different translations for better understanding:

"Now faith is the substance of the things hoped for, the evidence of things not seen." Hebrews 11:1 (KJV)

"Now faith is the assurance (title deed, confirmation) of things hoped for (divinely guaranteed), and the evidence of things not seen [the conviction of their reality—faith comprehends as fact what cannot be experienced by physical senses]." Hebrews 11:1 (AMP)

"What is faith? It is the confident assurance that something we want is going to happen. It is the certainty that what we hope for is waiting for us, even though we cannot see it up ahead." Hebrews 11:1 (LBV)

"Now faith is confidence in what we hope for and assurance about what we do not see." Hebrews 11:1 (NIV)

"Now faith is the assurance of things hoped for, the conviction of things not seen." Hebrews 11:1 (RSV)

By reading the above versions of this Bible passage, you can clearly see that faith is being sure of what you have not seen. Faith is seeing impossible things as possible. Faith is full assurance of God's ability to do whatever He says He will, even when our experiences look contrary to what He promised.

If a child wants to collect his school fees from his father and has not done anything that could make his father say no to his request, and he is also sure his father has the appropriate amount of money, he will be much bolder to state to anyone that he has a father who will pay his school fees. Even though he might not have even made the request yet from his father, he is so confident the money is available that all he needs to do is go home and make the request, and he will get the money. In the same way, this is how you should behave in your relationship with God as His child, because He is responsible for everything that you need and He has the answer to every one of your needs in His house. Therefore, come confidently and boldly to Him for your healing, without any doubt, and He will heal you.

God said to Noah that it will rain on the earth, though no rain ever had fallen. Noah was moved with faith and built an ark, as God had instructed him (Gen. 7:1–3). This action demonstrates Noah's confidence in the fact that because God said it will rain, then it would surely rain.

If you are coming to God for divine healing, then you must believe He is able to heal you and depend on Him for your healing. Remember, there is no part of your body that has a problem God doesn't have a solution to. He is the creator of every part of your body;

therefore, He has the ability to give you new parts when they are needed, the same way that every manufacturer has new parts for all of its products.

Hebrews 11:6 says:

> *"But without faith it is impossible to please him: for he that cometh to God must believe that he is, and that he is a rewarder of them that diligently seek him.*

> *"You can never please God without faith, without depending on Him. Anyone who wants to come to God must believe that there is a God and the He rewards those who sincerely look for him." (TLB)*

> *"But without faith it is impossible to [walk with God and] please Him, for whoever comes [near] to God must [necessarily] believe that God exists and that He rewards those who [earnestly and diligently] seek Him. (AMP)*

In fact, you cannot receive anything from God without faith. God is enough for all your needs in all areas of life, and the only way to receive things from God is to approach Him by faith.

How Does Faith Come?

Romans 10:17 says:

"So then faith cometh by hearing, and hearing by the word of God."

This is very important: faith is a product of what you hear. The main question is, what are you hearing? The words of men that talk about people who had the same sickness you had that are dead, or the Word of God that talks about God's power and willingness to heal you? You need to pay attention to the word of faith that will grant you healing.

The case of the woman with the issue of blood, in Mark 5:25–34, is a good reference for us on this subject. In verses 27 through 29 of this passage, we see that she said she had heard about Jesus:

"When she had heard of Jesus, came in the press behind, and touched his garment. For she said, If I may touch but his clothes, I shall be whole. And straightway the fountain of her blood was dried up; and she felt in her body that she was healed of that plague."

She heard about Jesus! That was the key—she had heard about how He healed the sick, raised the dead, cleansed the lepers, and cast out demons, and faith came alive in her because of what she had heard. So she said, in her heart, "It's my turn for healing," and decided to come and touch His clothes to get her healing; and she got it.

From this story, we learn that you need to hear the Word of God concerning your healing and develop your faith in the Word of God, and then you will receive anything you want from Him, as He promised in His word.

"[Jesus is] by whose stripes ye were healed.".
1 Peter 2:24b

The Word of God says by the stripes Jesus received two thousand years ago you have been healed. It is simply telling you that the sickness in your body is not there, because it has been healed. That is how God sees it, and you should see it like that with faith. Despite all the pains and symptoms of sickness in your body, God says you have been healed. With this heart of faith in God, step out of your sickbed and take a walk; and the healing will be perfected by your faith. You may say, "But Brother David, you don't really know how I feel about that. I have been trying but I cannot come out of it," and I will say, "Yes, I know, but the first step is to start imagining yourself out of that bed of sickness and taking a walk around. Do this over and over in faith, and it will work!"

> *"Himself took our infirmities, and bare our sicknesses." Matthew 8:17*

Let's learn a little bit of grammar here! The Bible says, *"[He] took,"* which is in past tense, proving that healing has already taken place and that He has taken it away. Now, *"our infirmities,"* which means that sickness in you has been taken away; this means that it is not with you anymore. To operate in faith, you only need to stand up and say, deep in your spirit, that you are somebody without sickness and infirmities; see yourself without any sickness and infirmities, and jump out of your bed perfectly and absolutely depending on God with full confidence in His word, and you will certainly be healed completely.

Faith is an action motivated by the Word of God; it is by nature evidential. If you can't see the evidence, then what you are referring to is not faith. James 2:18 says:

> *"Yea, a man may say, Thou hast faith, and I have works: shew me thy faith without thy works, and I will shew thee my faith by my works." James 2:18*

Faith without action is fake! That means it is dead (James 2:17). Faith is a reflective act. You can't operate it without it being seen. It shows in your looks and walk, in the statements you make, and in your countenance. For example, if you believe that *"by his stripes you are*

healed," you will not continue to lie in your bed. Faith is evident in the doing, the showing, and in the action.

Jesus said to those men at the wedding ceremony ***"Fill the waterpots with water" (John 2:7).*** They went ahead and did exactly as they were instructed, and the water became wine (John 2:1–11). There is no evidence of faith without the act. Action is the authentic evidence of faith. Faith is fake without backup action. If you want your healing now, faith is the key you need, and your healing will be granted in the name of Jesus. I pray now that the power of God penetrates your body, from head to toe, and that you receive your healing now in the name of Jesus.

As we continue in this adventure into the realm of the supernatural, I want you to be very sensitive because God is with you there, breathing the breath of life into your soul and restoring your peace and health back to you right now. Hear and see Him on the pages of this book, and receive your healings in the name of Jesus Christ.

"Death and life are in the power of the tongue: and they that love it shall eat the fruit thereof." Proverbs 18:21

Chapter Three
THE POWER OF CONFESSION

There is a strong authority in the mouth of every single human being, which has been imbibed in his tongue to create good or bad conditions for himself by choice. Proverbs 18:21 says:

> *"Death and life are in the power of the tongue: and they that love it shall eat the fruit thereof."*

We can see clearly in the above passage what your tongue carries and how you can benefit from it if you make good use of it. One major thing we use our tongues for, on a daily basis, is making confessions.

There are two type of confession: NEGATIVE and POSITIVE confessions.

Positive Confession

This type of confession is very important to the healing of your body, if you truly want to be healed. Positive confession is an open expression of faith in the power in God, in agreement with His words. This comes as a result of the level of your faith that you've drawn from the Word of God in your heart. Romans 10:10 says:

> *"For with the heart man believeth unto righteousness; and with the mouth confession is made unto salvation."*

There is always believing on the inside and speaking forth on the outside that give birth to the creative force of faith in us.

The Bible says, *"Let the weak say, I am strong" (Joel 3:10).*

This is a strong confession of faith. If a man is weak on the inside, but he believes God and he announces strength on the outside, in obedience to the Word of God, this action will surely give birth to divine strength in his body. Mark 11:23 tells us about the power of positive confession in moving a mountain:

> *"For verily I say unto you, That whoever shall say unto this mountain, Be thou removed, and be thou cast into the sea; and shall not doubt in his heart, but shall believe that those things which he saith shall come to pass; he shall have whatsoever he saith." Mark 11:23*

Brethren, believing in the heart and speaking with the mouth is what gives birth to the desired miracle in every area of life.

You must change your confession about yourself. So many people will just open their mouths and begin to announce negative things about themselves, such as: "I am always weak, I don't think I can survive this situation, etc." But you need to know what you say about your situation matters.

I know a man who has not had a single word of faith in his mouth. Though he has been prayed for by many people, many of them anointed men and women of God, and he himself always prays about his health, but every time he talks, the main subject of his discussion is how bad his health is and how serious the sickness is. He makes references to people who have suffered from the same sickness, and are now dead, and how he is just expecting death one day from this sickness. This has made his case grow worse because he has had no positive confessions in his mouth about the situation. Sometimes I wonder why people pray to be healed when they are expecting the sickness to kill them one day. I would say to them, "If you want to die, just expect death and you don't need to pray for healing, but if you want to live, pray and confess your healing, even if your body doesn't feel it yet."

***"For by thy words thou shall be justified,
and by thy words thou shalt be condemned."
Matthew 12:37***

It is your words that make you or mess you up. You've got to learn how to speak, so that you will not put yourself into problems daily by what you say about yourself.

NEGATIVE CONFESSION

This is a type of confession that you make affirming the operations of the devil in your life and recognizing the supremacy of the power of evil.

A man who is experiencing a headache opens his mouth and says, "I have a headache" has naturally given that feeling attention and made personal confession of having a headache. Therefore, his first though is to go and take medication or that he should go to the hospital. When he says, "I have a headache," he takes personal possession of the headache and it will stay with him. He can as well say, "I feel a headache," pray against it, and take some time to rest.

The devil is not a gentle spirit; he is very cunning and always likes to take what you say and use that against you to put you into a problem. That is why the Scripture says: ***"You are snared by the words of your mouth; You are taken by the words of your mouth" (Prov. 6:2, NKJV).***

Hear this: the sower went forth and sowed the seed. What was the seed? The word that was spoken!

"While the earth remaineth, seedtime and harvest.....shall not cease." Genesis 8:22

The words you speak are seeds waiting to harvest.

When you speak miracle words, it will never fail to bring you a miracle harvest. When you speak victory words, drawing strength from the Scripture, you have victory harvest. When you speak success words, you have success harvest. Until you can declare it, you will never possess it. The hidden force behind the triumphant saints is found in Mark 11:23:

> ***"Whosoever shall say [something,] . . . he shall have whatsoever he saith."***

Brethren, learn how to speak positive words unto yourself, so that all those negative words you speak will not finish you one day. What you release from your mouth will determine what you will see around you.

The almighty God gave us an example to follow at creation in chapter 1 of the book of Genesis, as He proclaimed what He wanted, saw all the things He had created, and pronounced that they were good.

In this chapter, the phrase *"And God said"* repeats from one verse to the next, beginning with the third verse and continuing in verses 6, 9, 11, 14, 20, 24, 26, and 29. But most of the outcome of those words He said are *"And God saw."* This shows us that what God said were the things that He saw.

If the almighty God follows the principle of speaking things into existence, how much more should you follow this principle? As you speak good things about yourself, you will see them coming to pass in your life. May the Lord teach you how to speak good things about yourself, so that you may see good things all the days of your life in Jesus's name.

Three things happen when you speak. Next, I will explain those three things so that you can have a better understanding of the power of confession.

God Backs What You Say

Let's look at the following phrase in Isaiah 44:26:

". . . that confirmeth the word of his servant, and performeth the counsel of his messengers."

God always backs your words when you say them in accordance with His word. When you say, "Thus saith the Lord" or "It is written," He says, "Yes, I said so, and when I say so, who can change My words? When I stretch forth My hand, who shall turn it back?" Rest assured that God will move into action to perform what you say in accordance with His words.

THE ANGELS ACT ON WHAT YOU SAY

"Suffer not thy mouth to cause thy flesh to sin; neither say thou before the angel, that it was an error: wherefore should God be angry at thy voice, and destroy the work of thy hands?" Ecclesiastes 5:6

Watch what you say; the angels stand at attention to carry out exactly what you say. You can't turn around and say, "I was just joking." Once you say it, they make it a reality.

SATAN BOWS AT YOUR WORD

No devil can stop the effect of your words when you open your mouth and proclaim things in accordance with God's Word for your life. Luke 21:15 says:

"For I will give you a mouth and wisdom, which all your adversaries shall not be able to gainsay nor resist."

No matter how strong the adversaries may be, they cannot withstand the power of your confession when you are producing it out of a deep revelation from God's Word. Until you open your mouth wide with Scripture, your enemies remain in charge. They cannot be subdued until you open your mouth wide and declare publicly what you are expecting.

Please stand on this: no matter what you feel in your body, don't say "I am sick," because what you say is what you will experience. Satan gives up on you if you speak the words of faith rather than those of sickness.

Do you want to live in perfect health? Don't talk of sickness. If you are sick in your body, begin to talk about healing and sound health, and you will surely have it.

"For she said within herself, If I may but touch his garment, I shall be whole."
Matthew 9:21

Chapter Four
YOU NEED A POINT OF CONTACT

———◆———

GOD IS A SPIRIT, AND SOMETIMES WE ARE confused because He is not directly before us in a human body. We cannot see Him with the human eye, and neither can we take a trip to heaven and present our case to Him, as we would if we were at our doctor's office.

How, then, can we reach Him? We can reach Him by using a point of contact. A point of contact is the means of sending your faith to God. A point of contact is something tangible, something you do, and when you do it, you release your faith toward God.

Your faith is the meeting ground between your limited self and your limitless God. A point of contact is given as a means of helping you to release your faith. Establishing a point of contact is like turning on the ignition key of your car and expecting something to happen in the car's engine realm.

The centurion who came to Jesus said, ***"Lord, I am not worthy that thou shouldest come under my*** *roof: but speak the word only, and my servant shall be healed" (Matt. 8:8).*

Speak the word!

He continued by saying: *"For I also am a man set under authority, having under me soldiers, and I say unto one, Go, and he goeth; and to another, Come, and he cometh; and to my servant, Do this and, he doeth it" (Luke 7:8).*

This Roman soldier was saying he recognizes authority and he's obedient to it. His master, Caesar, does not have to be present for his command to be carried out, because the power and the authority of the empire are vested in Caesar. This power has been delegated to the emperor's soldier; therefore, when the centurion gives an order to the soldier under him, the soldier obeys without question.

In this passage, the centurion was making Jesus understand that he knew Jesus had authority over his servant's sickness. He was saying to Jesus, "You don't need to come to my house; I am not worthy of such an honor. Just say a word, and my servant shall live, and I will believe and return home with assurance that he is well."

This is living faith—unquestioned, simple, childlike faith that believes in an honest and true way that God will send His power to accomplish whatsoever faith asks.

The Lord answered simply, *"Go thy way; and as thou hast believed, so be it done unto thee" (Matt. 8:13).*

♦ *You Need A Point Of Contact* ♦

And the centurion's servant was healed in the same hour! The centurion's point of contact was the spoken word from Jesus, who had all the power in heaven and on earth over all sicknesses and diseases. The moment Jesus spoke, the centurion released his faith and his servant was made whole. This is the master key to healing. The point of contact sets the time. The centurion's time for the healing of the servant was the moment Jesus spoke.

Remember that the woman with the issue of blood also used a point of contact, which helped her set the time for her healing. She said, *"If I may touch but his clothes, I shall be whole" (Mark 5:28).*

The book of the Acts of the apostles tells us how handkerchiefs or aprons were sent from the body of the apostle Paul to the sick and demon-possessed, and how through faith in the power of God, which they believed was available in the apostle Paul's clothes, healings were wrought. These clothes became a point of contact, and when they were placed upon the bodies of the sick and the afflicted, the sick and the afflicted released their faith and were set free.

Today, many lay their hands on their radios or their television sets as points of contact when healing ministers are preaching and praying for them; and they release their faith and, through faith, are healed during the radio or television outreaches.

Jesus is not here today with His seamless robe, nor Paul with his blessed clothes, nor Peter with his shadow that brought healing, but God has not left Himself without human instruments to deliver His power to us and get us out of our troubles. There are men and women of God who are gifted by the Holy Ghost to heal sicknesses and diseases, who through their laying on of hands, or through a point of contact, you can reach out with faith and be healed during their prayers.

I so believe in the ministry of laying on of hands that I lay my hands on people for healing during our healing services, so they will be healed by God through my empty hands; and many people have been healed through this wonderful point of contact as I pray for them.

Jesus said in Mark 16:17–18:

"And these signs shall follow them that believe; In my name shall they cast out devils, they shall speak with new tongues, they shall take up serpents, and if they drink any deadly thing, it shall not hurt them; they shall LAY HANDS ON THE SICK, and they shall RECOVER." (Emphasis added).

Laying of hands on the sick for healing is a fulfillment of this Bible passage. God has given so many people in the body of Christ the anointing to heal, and these people are in our midst day in and day out. We need only to get to them and make them our points of contact for divine healing, while we release our faith for healing.

> *"Is any sick among you? Let him call for the elders of the church; and let them pray over him, anointing him in the name of the Lord." James 5:14*

Elders in the above mentioned passage of the Bible are the spiritual leaders of the church—ministers such as pastors, evangelists, teachers, and deacons.

Friends, release your faith. Hang it on some biblical means of deliverance and allow God to meet you at the point of your need, as you receive your blessing of healing in Jesus's name.

In the next chapters, I wish to speak on some biblical points of contacts that you can release your faith in to get healed.

"Then Samuel took the horn of oil, and anointed him in the midst of his brethren: and the Spirit of the Lord came upon David from that day forward."
1 Samuel 16:13

Chapter Five
THE ANOINTING OIL

WHAT IS THE ANOINTING OIL? IT IS VERY important to know what the anointing oil is before learning what it can do in healing the sick.

With my level of understanding of the anointing oil, I want to define it as the medium by which the Holy Spirit is being invoked to intervene on behalf of humankind. For example, when David was anointed in the book of Samuel, the Bible describes it this way:

> ***"Then Samuel took the horn of oil, and anointed him in the midst of his brethren: and the Spirit of the Lord came upon David from that day forward." 1 Samuel 16:13***

What brought the Spirit of God upon David was the anointing oil. The anointing oil communicates the personality of the Holy Spirit of God, for His direct, personal intervention. When the anointing oil is applied, the Holy Spirit will show up. Through the medium of the anointing oil, the beneficiary can enjoy the supernatural ministry of the Holy Spirit. The Holy Spirit goes all out to prove that He is the finger of God. In fact, no situation can be above the Holy Spirit, and no challenges of life will be more than what the Spirit of God can handle.

The anointing oil has its roots in the Old Testament and is confirmed in the New Testament, at the time of Jesus's ministry on the surface of the earth. Also, the apostle James, in his letter to the body of Christ, confirms the usefulness of the anointing oil.

God gave detailed instruction to Moses for the mixing of the anointing oil in Exodus 30:23–31. The details that God gave shows He must have something spectacular in His mind for introducing the ministry of the anointed oil.

Jesus Christ was completely against sicknesses and diseases, and He proved it during the time of His ministry on the surface of the earth. Serious study of the Gospels show that Jesus did three important things during His time:

- ➢ Preach the gospel
- ➢ Cast out devils
- ➢ Heal the sick

These were also the assignments that He committed into the hands of His disciples when He sent them out both during His human lifetime and after His resurrection and ascension.

The disciples made use of the anointing oil to heal the sick when Jesus sent them out to preach:

"And they went out, and preached that men should repent. And they cast out many devils, and anointed with OIL many that were SICK, and HEALED them." Mark 6:12–13 (emphasis added)

Now, who gave them the oil? I can say it was Jesus, who sent them forth and gave it to them. He gave them the oils as a solution for sicknesses and diseases. And they used it, thus showing that it wasn't just an Old Testament ritual.

James, as one of the apostles, understood what Jesus taught them when He was with them during his earthly ministry and recommended the same thing for any sick person in his letter:

"Is any sick among you? Let him call for the elders of the church; and let them pray over him, anointing him with oil in the name of the Lord. And the prayer of faith shall save the sick, and the Lord shall raise him up; and if he have committed sins, they shall be forgiven him." James 5:14–15

The anointing oil is so strong that it can heal any kind of sickness and disease. I have seen someone healed of cancer through the application of the anointing oil. There is hope of divine healing for anybody, if they believe God and have faith in the power of God through the ministry of the anointing oil.

The anointing oil can heal the sick with the prayer of faith. Note this point very well: it is not the prayer of doubt, but the PRAYER OF FAITH that can heal the sick with the anointing oil.

The application of faith in any spiritual thing matters most if you want to get a result from God about it. Therefore, if you want to use the anointing oil for healing and you have faith in God (not in the oil—because the oil has no power of its own), then it will surely work because God will grant your request.

There is no sickness or disease of any kind that can escape the power of God in the anointing oil. Here are some living proofs:

- There was an old woman who was having eye problems and could not see clearly because of her age. I was called upon to pray for her, and I went to visit her with the anointing oil. I anointed her eyes with the oil, prayed for her, and left for home. On the second day after I had seen her, she called me and explained to me how she had a surgical operation done by some unseen people in the night on her eyes and that now she could see clearly like a baby. I surely believed that she must have experienced angelic visitation after the prayer and the anointing of her eyes with oil. What a great God we serve!

- After a brother complained to me of a serious headache, which had been disturbing him for some months, I told him to anoint his head with the oil we had prayed over at the church and rebuke the headache; he did so, and the headache vanished completely.
- A woman was sick and had been carried to the hospital for treatments, but the medical doctors could not determine her real problem after a series of tests. At that point, her sister came to the church and explained that the devil had afflicted her. I told the sister to bring me a bottle of olive oil, and after I prayed over it in the name of Jesus, she took it to the hospital and anointed her sister on the head with it. To the glory of God, the woman was completely healed on the second day and was discharged from the hospital that evening.

There are many healings that I have seen God do through the ministry of the anointing oil, of which space will not permit me to write about here. If you are sick, you can call on your pastor to pray for you with the anointing oil, or any of the leaders in your church that you know has a relationship with God, to help you pray over the oil and anoint yourself with it in the name of Jesus; and you shall be healed. If you have faith in God, God can heal you through this point of contact. It works!

"And he took bread, and gave thanks, and brake it, and gave unto them, saying, This is my body which is given for you: this do in remembrance of me." Luke 22:19

Chapter Six
THE COMMUNION OF HEALING

THE HOLY COMMUNION, OR THE BREAKING of bread and the drinking of wine that represent the body and the blood of our Lord Jesus Christ, was given to us by our Lord Jesus Christ Himself before He left the surface of the earth.

This is very important to the church because it is one of the three important services that Jesus our Lord gave us and led us to do in the church.

> ***"And he took bread, and gave thanks, and brake it, and gave unto them, saying, this is my body which is given for you: this do in remembrance of me." Luke 22:19***

As you can see in the above passage, it was Jesus Himself who gave the practice of Holy Communion to the church as an order that must be followed. Through deep revelation of the Holy Spirit, we have been able to discover that the mystery of the Holy Communion carries strong power to heal believers in Christ Jesus, and also to deliver them from and break demonic strongholds in their lives.

In this chapter, we want to see how powerful the mystery of the Holy Communion is in the area of healing in the body of Christ, which is the church, and how we can enjoy the blessing therein in getting our healing.

> *Then Jesus said unto them, "Verily, verily, I say unto you, Except ye eat the flesh of the Son of man and drink his blood, ye have no life in you." John 6:53*

The power of God resides in the body and the blood of Jesus. Remember, the life of any animal is in its blood. Therefore, when you take the blood of Jesus, in the form of the communion wine, and His body, in the form of bread, you are impacting the power that resides in His body into your body to heal you. Through the breaking of bread, or communion service, we are made to eat His flesh and drink His blood so that everything in Christ may be transferred into our bodies, souls, and spirits.

> *"But he was wounded for our transgressions, he was bruised for our iniquities: the chastisement of our peace was upon him; and with his stripes we are healed." Isaiah 53:5*

One of the reasons Jesus bled when He was beaten with a scourge was to make provision for our healing. In the above passage, we are made to understand that it is by the stripes He received on His body that we are healed.

Therefore, when you are taking His blood, you are appropriating the healing virtue into your body that came out of Him through the stripes on His body. This works against any sickness that is in your body and brings divine healing He has already paid for into your own body, and by this process, you will receive your own healing.

I am a living testimony of the healing that is available through the communion service.

There was a time that I was involved in an auto crash and I subsequently developed chest pain as a result of the crash, which later resulted in pneumonia. I took a lot of medications and began to use hot water and hot food, but the problem persisted. One day, I was in the church during the communion service, and the pastor was preaching on healing as we took our communion. As I listened to him, I believed and set my heart on this problem of mine and took this wonderful communion for my healing. To the glory of God, that was the end of that sickness in my life, and now I can drink cold water — something I couldn't do before — any time I want to cool my thirst.

Your healing is possible if you can have faith in God to use this point of contact. In fact, your faith is much more important than anything else that will lead to your healing. If you read your Bible carefully, you will discover that many people who came to Jesus during His earthly ministry for healing operated in faith for them to receive their healing. To some of them, Jesus simply said, *"Thy FAITH has made you whole" (Matt. 9: 22. Luke 17:19).*

Therefore, it is very important for you to come to the communion table with strong faith for your healing. As you approach the table for your healing, with strong faith, the power of God that resides in communion for healing will flow into your life and bring you the healing that you need in Jesus's name.

I have received many testimonies from people who were healed through the communion table, which shows the tremendous power of God in it. I will share the following two testimonies for you to see how God has worked tremendously in the lives of people through the communion service.

I was seriously sick for many years, and I was carried to different hospitals for treatment, but none were able to discover my problem or solve it for me, so I was carried back home. After that, the pastor came to our house to pray for me, and he served me the Holy Communion on the bed right there in my room. Two days later, an unknown strength come into my body so that I became much stronger and stood up and walked from one corner of the house to the other. That was how my healing started. After that, the pastor came to my house and served me the communion every day for about one week, and I was completely healed from my sickness.

David T.A. Lagos, Nigeria.

I had diabetes for about three years, but one day I was in the church during a communion service where the pastor had been invited to preach on divine healing. Faith was built in me through the word of God, and I received the communion with faith that day, and continued to take the communion on my own every day for two months. By the time I went for my next checkup, my A1c was 6.5, down from 8.9 the previous visit. God healed me of my sickness. After that, I made the communion a regular practice in my household, and God has been very faithful to His word. In fact, it is because God is so faithful and good that I was healed.

Adeyemi C.O. Atlanta, Georgia

You too can be healed through this wonderful mystery. It works!

"For an angel went down at a certain season into the pool, and troubled the water: whosoever then first after the troubling of the water stepped in was made whole of whatsoever disease he had." John 5:4

Chapter Seven
THE HEALING WATER

———◆◆◆———

HEALING WATER IS ONE OF THE POWERFUL points of contact I have seen being used in Africa, most especially in Nigeria, for healing. Late Apostle Ayo Babalola, the founding apostle of the Christ Apostolic Church and the first general evangelist of the same denomination worldwide, made use of the "healing water" as a very strong point of contact for healing in his days of great revival in Nigeria. I heard that this man of God operated in a unique healing anointing; as he blessed the water for the sick people, and gave it to them to drink and to bathe in, many people were recorded to have received healings through this point of contact.

The healing water is a Bible-based means of divine healing, and we can read how God performed many healings through water in the Scripture.

The healing of Naaman the leper in 2 Kings 5:1–15 is one example of healing through water, and the pool of Bethesda in chapter 5 of the Gospel of John is another example of healing through water. I have seen this means of healing being used even before I became born again. I remember when a child was sick in our area. This child was ill to the extent that the doctor said he could do nothing to save his life, and he gave the child only a few days to live. Hearing this, his parents carried him to the traditional healers, who also were not able to do anything about his case. Therefore, he was later carried to a church where the pastor prayed on a bowl of water and told his parents to bath the child with the water, and also to give him some to drink.

Within seven days, the boy was healed so dramatically by the power of God, and the pastor said they should take him home and continue to use that same water for him; and that when the water was finished, they should get more water and give it to any genuine man of God to pray over it, so that they could continue using it for the child until he was completely whole. To the glory of God, without using any medication again, except this water, the child was completely healed. Growing up later, I found out that the pastor who prayed over the water was one of the pastors from the Christ Apostolic Church, founded by Apostle Ayo Babalola. This was the beginning of my understanding about the healing water.

So many times, in our programs too, people have brought water for us to pray over the water for their healing during my traveling ministry, and we've recorded many testimonies of God using this point of contact for His people to get their healings, as people released their faith and get healed of their sicknesses.

The Healing Water

So, if you have faith in receiving healing through this point of contact (healing water), reach out to God as you make use of it, and you will receive your healing in Jesus's name.

"And God wrought special miracles by the hand of Paul: So that from his body were brought unto the sick handkerchiefs or aprons, and the diseases departed from them, and the evil spirits went out of them." Acts 19:11–12 (KJV)

Chapter Eight
THE HEALING MANTLE

THE HEALING MANTLE IS ANOTHER STRONG point of contact that has been in existence since the time of the apostles.

> *"And God wrought special miracles by the hand of Paul: So that from his body were brought unto the sick handkerchiefs and aprons, and the diseases departed from them, and the evil spirits went out of them."*
> *Acts 19:11–12*

The healing mantle has been a strong point of contact for healing and deliverances in the church of God, most especially at the time the church experienced it during the time of the apostle Paul.

It is not the cloth of the people that are being taken from them that heals, but the power of God that comes upon that cloth and the faith of the people using it as a point of contact for their healing.

I have heard so many testimonies from people about the healing mantle, but my faith became stronger in it the day I heard a personal testimony about it regarding my handkerchief. It all happened when I was invited to an institution of higher learning in Osun State, Nigeria, to preach the word during a special student fellowship program. On the second day of the program, a lady came to me with a handkerchief and requested my own handkerchief in exchange for the one she had brought. I first felt reluctant about her request, but I didn't feel any restriction in my spirit, so I released my handkerchief and collected hers in exchange.

Two months later, I was invited to preach by another fellowship at the same institution. When this lady heard that I was in town to preach, she came to me and explained how she had been delivered from a serious menstrual pain that had been afflicting her for almost six years. She said the pain had been so serious, she had been carried from one hospital to the other any time she was experiencing it. A lot of medications and charms had been prescribed and given to her by medical and native doctors, but she could not be relieved of the pain. She also said that the day she had come to collect my handkerchief was just two days before her menstrual period, and that she had already started feeling the pain by then, although it was not yet as serious as it usually became on the real day of menstruation.

She told me that after taking the handkerchief, she had laid it on her stomach and prayed, invoking the healing anointing on the handkerchief to heal her. That was all she could tell me of the story before she burst into tears of joy for having been healed of this serious pain by the power of God. I was so happy for her and so excited about this experience that my faith grew in the use of this point of contact, and I have since ministered to people in our anointing and healing meetings through this point of contact as the Holy Spirit leads. Now we have many testimonies attesting to God's power being demonstrated through this point of contact to divine healing.

The healing mantle is still a strong point of contact today, and you can just release your faith through this means to God and be given your healing.

I wish to say this also: Any material being used by the anointed men and women of God, and any material prayed over by them, could be used as a point of contact, if you release your faith to God and believe that the anointed man or woman really is a prophet of God.

"Hear me, O Judah, and ye inhabitants of Jerusalem; Believe in the Lord your God, so shall ye be established; believe his prophets, so shall ye prosper." 2 Chronicles 20:20

You need to believe God and believe the prophet of God that God is sending your way for your healing.

So many people only believe God for divine healing, but they don't believe in the prophet of God He is sending their way for their healing. If you don't believe a man or woman of God, the anointing of God on him or her will never work for you, no matter the level of your faith in God. If you don't believe in the man or woman of God who is to pray for your healing, then it is better for you to pray for your healing yourself in your own room than to go to a man or woman of God whom you don't believe.

Connect your faith with God by any of these points of contact discussed in this book, and your healing will come your way in Jesus's name.

"In those days was Hezekiah sick unto death. And the prophet Isaiah the son of Amoz came to him, and said unto him, Thus saith the LORD, Set thine house in order; for thou shalt die, and not live. Then he turned his face to the wall, and prayed unto the LORD, saying, I beseech thee, O LORD, remember now how I have walked before thee in truth and with a perfect heart, and have done that which is good in thy sight. And Hezekiah wept sore." 2 Kings 20:1-3

Chapter Nine
PRAYING FOR DIVINE HEALING

YOU CAN PRAY PERSONALLY FOR YOUR healing, and you will be healed. I would like to share with you about prayer for healing from the Bible. Let's look to 2 Kings 20:1–6 to read about a man who prayed himself out of sickness and death:

> *"In those days was Hezekiah sick unto death. And the prophet Isaiah the son of Amoz came to him, and said unto him, Thus saith the LORD, Set thine house in order; for thou shalt die, and not live. Then he turned his face to the wall, and prayed unto the LORD, saying, I beseech thee, O LORD, remember now how I have walked before thee in truth and with a perfect heart, and have done that which is good in thy sight. And Hezekiah wept sore." 2 Kings 20:1–3*

> *"Thus said the LORD, the God of David thy father, I have heard thy prayer; I have*

> *seen thy tears: behold, I will heal thee: . . .*
> *. And I will add to thy days fifteen years[.]"*
> *2 Kings 20:5–6*

The initial message that God sent to Hezekiah was a message of death, and this triggered him to pray a very serious prayer that led to his healing and deliverance from death. If you are sick, you don't have to wait until you hear the message of death before you begin to pray. You can speak directly to God for your healing, telling him how painful your situation is and asking for His power of healing to come upon you and heal you completely.

> *"For we have not a High Priest which cannot be touched with the feeling of our infirmities . . . ." Hebrews 4:15*

Suppose you pray and apparently there is no response whatsoever from God as you expected; this means God does not answer prayers indiscriminately.

Jesus has given us an example of this: He told the story of a widow who was unjustly treated and went to state her case before a judge. The judge listened impatiently to her story and said, "Come back later." But this woman persisted in returning to the judge to request his help until the judge knew not what to do other than to answer her request (Luke 18:1-5).

The Lord said that the unjust judge then avenged the woman of her adversaries, not because he sympathized with her case but because she persuaded him into action by her unrelenting demands. Now hear what the Lord said in verses 7 and 8:

> *"And shall not God avenge his own elect, which cry day and night unto him, though he bear long with them? I tell you that he will avenge them speedily. Nevertheless, when the Son of man cometh, shall he find faith on the earth?" Luke 18:7–8*

If the unjust judge helps a woman only because of her insistence, how much more will God, who is in sympathy with our causes, help those who come to him with determination and faith to receive their requests from Him?

In other words, if, when you pray to God, you have any thought of giving up before an answer comes, your prayer will doubtlessly go unanswered.

This indicates the kind of people whose prayer God answers. If you have a quitter's spirit, God will let you quit. Remember that quitters don't win and winners don't quit; your prayer is only as strong as the attitude that backs it up.

Therefore, if there seems to be no answer for your prayers, God might be seeking to change and improve the kind of person you are by causing you to reexamine yourself to see if you have the right attitude and desire; and whether you will have the power and fortitude to stand in His presence persistently and not quit.

In the Gospel of Matthew 15:21–28, when Jesus told a woman who came begging for healing that He was not sent but to the lost sheep of the house of Israel, He was saying no to her prayer but not necessarily to her as a person. Before His conversation with her was over, even though He had first said no, He ended up giving her what she wanted—healing for her child—because she had persisted and decided not to care about any funny thing that Jesus said to her.

Most of the time, when God answers NO, He has a better way. He doesn't mean no in the sense that people do. God's refusal is subject to change when we conform ourselves to His will and do what is ultimately best for us.

When God answers no, it does not mean that we are completely cut off from Him but that we now have the opportunity to examine ourselves and discover if we really want our healing on God's terms or only on our own terms. So many people come to God in prayer for healing and yet, deep inside themselves, they still hold hope of many other alternatives to their healing.

It is those who come to God sincerely and are absolutely depending on God, and God only, who deserve answers from Him, not the people who believe they still have other means or options for their healings.

There is another kind of situation that God uses for His own glorification: sometimes, what seems to be the present NO from God is simply because He will be answering the prayer later, in His own time and for His own glorification. This kind of situation is found in the story of Lazarus, the brother of Mary and Martha (John 11:1–45). When Lazarus fell sick and his sisters sent for Jesus, the messenger said to Him, *"[B]ehold, He whom thou lovest is sick" (John 11:3).* When Jesus heard this message, He said:

> *"This sickness is not unto death, but for the glory of God, that the Son of God may be glorified thereby." John 11:4*

We see in this passage that Jesus said no to the request for Lazarus's healing, even though it was clear Jesus loved Martha, her sister Mary, and Lazarus. Despite this love for them, He spent two days where He was and did not return to the town of Lazarus until Lazarus was dead and had been buried for four days. When the messenger had asked for Lazarus's healing, Jesus had told him that Lazarus's sickness was to glorify God. Now we see that this was because Jesus intended to raise Lazarus from the dead! Raising him from the dead would glorify God more than healing him. As this story demonstrates, God said no here to glorify Himself.

When Jesus got to Lazarus's grave, He said:

> ***"And I knew that thou hearest me: but because of the people which stand by I said it, that they may believe that thou hast sent me. And when he had thus spoken, he cried with a loud voice, Lazarus, come forth. . . . Loose him and let him go." John 11:42–44***

After Lazarus had been called forth from the grave, it was said, ***"Then many of the Jews which come to Mary, and had seen the things which Jesus did, believed on him" (John 11: 45).*** Also speaking of Lazarus being alive again, the Bible stated:

> ***"[By reason] of [Lazarus's resurrection by Jesus,] many of the Jews went away, and believed on Jesus." John 12:11***

As shown in this story, when it seems to you as if God is saying no in your case or that there is a delay, it might mean that God has a better way to glorify Himself in your case. Only continue to believe God, and you will surely have a way out at the end of everything, and the glory will return to God.

"How God anointed Jesus of Nazareth with the Holy Ghost and with power: who went about doing good, and healing all that were oppressed of the devil, for God was with him." **Acts 10:38**

Chapter Ten
SEVEN RULES OF FAITH FOR DIVINE HEALING

YEARS AGO, I HEARD A MESSAGE PREACHED by the late Oral Roberts, one of the men whom God has strongly used in the healing ministry around the world through a cassette tape given to me by a friend. In that message, I discovered some powerful steps of faith for divine healing that I have shared with people trusting God for divine healing and it has worked for many in getting their healing. I later discovered that these same principles of divine healing were shared in his book titled *"If You Need Healing Do These Things."*

Those principles I discovered from that message are very important steps I know will bless you and help you in seeking divine healing and I will love to share them with you in this book.

He shared the story from the book of 2 Kings 5:1–15 about General Naaman of Syria, a general in Syria's expeditionary forces. Because of General Naaman's outstanding military success, he had been hailed as a national hero and was well respected by everybody in Syria. Despite the greatness of this man in the military forces, however, he had leprosy, a terrible disease that was widely prevalent in those days.

Leprosy meant a living death—slow, torturous, isolated suffering. This disease is a foul and inhuman thing, and is not numbered among the blessings of life. Jesus Christ came against it in the power of His pure and healthy humanity, laying His healing hands upon the sick and tormented people with leprosy and healing them.

In the story of Naaman's miraculous healing through his faith in God, there are seven rules of faith that Reverend Roberts laid out that we can use today for our healing. I will list them here, as stated by him in that message.

ONE: Recognize that Sicknesses and Diseases Are Oppressions of the Devil.

This rule of faith was made clear to us by the apostle Peter, the man who knew the Savior's love for suffering humanity. After the resurrection of Christ, when the apostle was preaching to the soldiers in the house of Cornelius in Caesarea, he said:

> *"How God anointed Jesus of Nazareth with the Holy Ghost and with power: who went about doing good, and healing all that were oppressed of the devil; for God was with him." Acts 10: 38*

"Healing all that were oppressed of the devil": this was Peter's summation of the ministry of the Lord Jesus. Peter said Satan is a destroyer of human life, while Jesus is a destroyer of the oppressions of the devil.

The four Gospels tell the story of Jesus and His healing power. All of them tell how Jesus found the people oppressed with all manner of sicknesses and diseases and healed them all. They all speak of how compassion flowed through Him, like the water of a pure mountain stream and became healing water for all who would believe (John 4:14). The healing water of Jesus is God's antidote against disease and is available now to all who have faith in Him.

Jesus did not turn away any person who had faith. Making no differentiation as to race or gender, He looked for faith, and wherever He found it, He caused healing to take place. One of His favorite expressions was:

"[A]s thou hast believed, so be it done unto thee." Matthew 8:13

He healed the blind, the deaf, the crippled, the demon-possessed, the feverish, the brokenhearted, and many others. Those afflicted were classified by the apostle Peter as being oppressed. He saw that these oppressed people were healed by the Master.

Healing power was given to the followers of Jesus Christ, and many of them were outstandingly successful in healing the people (Matt. 10:1). For example, Peter's shadow was used as a point of contact for healing people upon whom it fell (Acts 5:15). Similarly, Stephen and Philip, laymen of the early church through faith, brought outstanding healing to many oppressed people (Acts 6:8, Acts 8:5–8). Jesus had glorious success in healing the souls, minds, and bodies of the multitudes. He never said to one person, "It is not My will to heal you" and to another "It is My will to heal you"; instead, He healed all those who were oppressed of the devil, and who believed in Him and His power to heal them.

This means that in the use of His miraculous power, He requires faith in those who would be healed. His deep concern that is spoken about in the Scripture is traceable not only to the sin of mankind, but also to the unbelief of the people He came to deliver.

The power of God to heal human life is still active today in all churches and in all walks of life, through the faith and love of His people. God honors the faith and love of His people, for their faith and love honor God.

If we go back to the story of Naaman in 2 Kings, we read that he had made a victorious march across the land of Israel, and some other countries of his time, and had taken many captives. One of these captives was a little girl who had become a servant of Naaman's wife. This girl was familiar with God and His prophets and knew they could heal. Knowing that the general was a leper, she said:

"Would God my Lord were with the prophet that is in Samaria [Israel]! For he would recover him of his leprosy." 2 Kings 5:3

Naaman was grateful for this hope, believed the little girl's message and made preparation to leave for Samaria at once. This leads us to the second rule:

TWO: Believe the Message.

The message of hope for Naaman came from a servant girl. The message of God is more important than its messenger. Oh, that all of us would believe this. We are becoming so denominationalized that we want to determine if God's messenger is a member of our denomination or church before we accept their message. We have lost sight of the importance of the message because of our insistence that the message carry our own label. God does not place the same stress upon our different theological emphases that we do. In becoming narrow-minded and bigoted in our theologies and creeds, we place ourselves in the same positions as the disciples who were sternly rebuked by Christ for their attempts to exclude outsiders from performing miracles in His name:

"And John answered him, saying, Master, we saw one casting out devils in thy name, and he followeth not us: and we forbade him, because he followeth not us. But Jesus

> *said, Forbid him not: for there is no man which do a miracle in my name, that can lightly speak evil of me." Mark 9:38–39*

This is Christ's indictment against sectarianism. It has been my experience that God does not compel us all to wear the same denomination label but, rather, that we love one another and work together to win souls.

The little Jewish girl said, *"Would God my Lord were with the prophet that is in Samaria! For he would recover him of his leprosy." 2 Kings 5:3*

Naaman heard the message and believed it; then he stepped forward to act on it. The message of Naaman's story for us today is that we need to believe the message of healing that is being preached to us, and follow the instructions in it for our healing to become a reality.

THREE: Go to Where the Power Is.

In the story of Naaman, the land of Israel represented God, and Elisha, who lived there, was God's prophet. Syria was a land of idol worshippers, and the message to Naaman was that he must get away from his old haunts of sin and get closer to God. In directing Naaman to "go to where the power is," the little girl was saying, "Go back to God, back to your moral vows and saving religion."

This may come as a shock to you, but you may have to change your entire way of life: your thoughts, your attitudes, your purposes, your religion, and your goals.

Why? Because if any part of your life is not on God's side, you must change it to get over to God's side, as that is where all you need can be found.

Naaman acted on the advice of the little maid and set forth on his trip to the land of Israel. But he made a serious mistake; instead of going to the prophet as advised, he went to the king of Israel. The king was distraught at being expected to heal Naaman when he knew that he did not have the power to do so and declared that he could do nothing for him.

> *"And it was so, when Elisha the man of God had heard that the king of Israel had rent his clothes, that he sent to the king, saying, Wherefore has thou rent thy clothes? Let him come now to me, and he shall know that there is a prophet in Israel." 2 Kings 5:8*

This is important, for it has to do with the next rule:

FOUR: Put Your Faith in God, Not Man.

The little girl had clearly told her master Naaman that the prophet would teach him how to use his faith to be healed of leprosy. Instead, he had gone to the king. I cannot insist too strongly that you put your faith in God. Have confidence in His servant or prophet, but put your faith in God, not man. The person whom God has chosen to help you receive your healing is an instrument, only the means to an end. Your deliverance is by faith in God and His power only.

After having been refused by the king, Naaman rode to the house of Elisha and sent his servant to announce his arrival. Having been forewarned by God that Naaman's attitude had to be changed, and discerning the general's pride and arrogance, the prophet acted accordingly, as we will see shortly.

Elisha was the servant of God—the human instrument only. He was in the delicate position of having to deal with a proud, dying man and having to govern his acts according to the rules of faith. Faith had to be aroused in Naaman; otherwise, he would have returned home with his leprosy. To be healed, a man's heart must be right with God and his soul in line with his maker. God, not the prophet or the preacher, is the healer. An attitude of selfishness, pride, and stubbornness makes it impossible for faith to be fully released. When God's minister is being used of God to help you, let wrong attitudes give way to love, making it possible for you to be healed by the power of God.

With great detachment, Elisha remained in his house. He sent the famous general a message by his servant: "Sir, the prophet said you should go and dip yourself seven times in the Jordan River, and your flesh shall be clean." Naaman was astonished, then enraged, and finally decided to return home. As Naaman went away, he muttered, "Go dip in the filthy river of Jordan? In fact, I though the prophet would at least come to me and do some great thing and heal me. If I had wanted to bathe, I would have stayed at home. At least the water in the river of Syria is clean."

Pride has stopped many people from receiving their healing from God, because they never think that when they ask for healing from God, they are not dealing with a man but with God, and that there are rules that govern faith. Humility; respect for God's message and His prophets; a desire to give up sin and to worship the true God—these are all attitudes that help a man get in harmony with God.

Thank God that Naaman's servant had a very good reasoning ability. He had to advise Naaman to stay and do as the prophet had suggested, or else he would have returned home the same way he had come—still afflicted with leprosy.

So many people come to God during healing services and programs and then return home the same way they came into the service, because they wanted God to heal them of their problems but still continued to focus on themselves rather than on God.

The servant said: ***"My father, if the prophet had bid thee do some great thing, wouldest thou not have done it? How much rather then, when he said to thee, wash and be clean? 2 Kings 5:13***

If you want divine healing, you need to put your faith in God totally and simply obey the instruction given to you by the prophet or the preacher for your healing to come.

FIVE: Accept the Correction of God.

Naaman listened, and when the servant had finished, he nodded his head in agreement. "You are right," he said. "I am wrong. I did come here self-centered and proud. Ah, this Elisha is a great prophet; he saw right through me. And his God must have shown the prophet the kind of man I am. 'Go dip yourself in Jordan,' the prophet says. Surely I can do that!"

It takes a humble spirit for one to change like that, and it is a marvelous thing when someone accepts God's correction in this way. It doesn't take long for a man to change if he wants to, but he must want to. When Naaman accepted God's correction, the Spirit of Christ entered him, and he became "a new creature."

Repentance is a change of mind before it becomes a change of heart. Naaman changed his mind and obeyed the prophet, and this brought his long-awaited change of the body. Simple obedience can bring great deliverance to people.

SIX: Lose Yourself.

What a contrast! The man who went to the wrong place for healing, who was rude to God's prophet, who was built by his own pride, who was a very angry man, who refused to obey, was now losing himself.

There are a lot of things that will be happening to us that we will not have the ability to overcome, if we don't lose ourselves in obedience to God and His word. Losing ourselves in obedience to God, knowing ourselves to be joined with the limitless power of Christ, and getting in line with the Savior are the things that count most when we seek to be healed through faith in God.

Naaman had come a long way since he had left Syria. Who would have believed the national hero would be dipping himself in a river? But as he was dipping himself into that river, he was enjoying every moment of it.

Something was going on in Naaman's spirit. He was joyously willing to take the sevenfold bath, even though he believed that he would be cured anyway. This step leads to the last and most important rule of all:

SEVEN: Use a Point of Contact.

The prophet Elisha had said that if Naaman would dip seven times in the river, his flesh would be cleansed from leprosy. What was this? Just a point of contact or a means through which he could release his faith? He was to dip seven times—no more, no less—in a designated river. The reason for having Naaman do this was that he would find by the time he became willing to do this, he would be in the right attitude, the proper frame of mind, to believe for a miraculous recovery.

He says, "Now I see it all. This is to prepare me for believing that God will heal me." He dips once, twice, thrice... and up to the seventh time. "Just this seventh time, and it will be done. I know God will heal me." In a like manner, your point of contact could be several things: it could be the laying on of hands or the use of anointing oil, the blessed handkerchief or healing water. It does not matter what the point of contact is—if it helps you release your faith, the healing will take place.

Naaman came out of this water the seventh time thinking, "I've done it! I've obeyed! Now the God of Israel will heal me." With unhampered faith in a limitless God, he walked out of the river bank, believing his leprosy would go. He had done what the prophet said. He had brought himself into harmony with God. He released his faith and . . . it happened.

> *"[A]nd his flesh came again like unto the flesh of a little child, and he was clean." 2 Kings 5:14*

He was so grateful that he returned to the prophet's house, but, as befits all true servants of God, Elisha would accept no gift for the miracle done. The general made his vows to the true God that he would worship Him and, henceforth, would serve no other gods. What a fitting climax! He obeyed the rules of faith and found a new life. But he did not forget God who had healed him. His leprosy was gone, and God had come into his life.

What God did for Naaman, He can do for you. If you follow these rules and release your faith, you will receive your healing.

"My son, attend to my words; incline thine ear unto my sayings. Let them not depart from thine eyes; keep them in the midst of thine heart. For they are life unto those that find them, and health to all their flesh." Proverbs 4:20–22

Chapter Eleven
MAINTAINING DIVINE HEALTH

DIVINE HEALTH IS A PROGRAM FROM GOD for every one of His children. There is no shortcut to divine health than to follow the basic rules to it. God has done everything possible for you to be in good health; that is why Jesus came to this world. God is not the author of sickness; the devil is, and he is planning and devising new diseases and releasing them into the world. You need to know your right to good health and insist on it.

You need to get acquainted with the rules and ways of God for handling every situation that you find yourself in. You can get this through studying and hearing the Word of God. This will be your anchor in life. God did not create you to be a struggler; He created you to be a victor. For you to maintain your health, you must keep your faith alive. Have victory mentality; let the Word of God become your identity. Be willing to take the word as you receive it from God; it will bring faith into you, and faith in you will get you anything you need from God. Following are six ways to maintain divine health:

1. FAITH

Your faith must constantly be at work; never ever relax your faith. It is your direct weapon against the devil. Faith is what you use in quenching all the fiery darts of the devil.

> *"Be sober, be vigilant; because your adversary the devil, as a roaring lion, walketh about seeking whom he may devour: whom resist steadfast in the faith . . . ." 1 Peter 5:8–9*

Do not wait for a disease to occur before putting your faith to work. Be in faith always and confess God's Word in faith, for that is one way you can keep sickness off your body permanently.

2. LOVE

Love is very important; in fact, you need a large heart to love the brethren. This will work to your own advantage; you will not lose anything by loving everybody around you. Everybody who is acceptable to God should be acceptable to you too. Love will help you to overcome a lot of difficulties in your life.

> *"We know that we have passed from death unto life, because we love the brethren. He that loveth not his brother abideth in death. Whosoever hateth his brother is a*

murderer: and ye know that no murderer hath eternal life abiding in him." 1 John 3:14–15

Hatred, malice, backbiting, and all sorts of similar negative traits and activities are products of lack of love, and you can't indulge in any of them and still remain in good health. In fact, your heart gets disturbed anytime you see somebody you hate, and be sure that whatever touches your heart will affect your health. Therefore, live and walk in love always.

3. FASTING

Fasting is another practice that keeps your health alive. Many Christians think that fasting is optional; Jesus did not give us that impression. He said, *"When you fast,"* not *"If you fast" (Matt. 6:16)* This means that fasting is for every believer. It is part of the Christian walk. There are times you must deliberately cease feeding your body so that you can take time to attend to spiritual matters. God Himself chose fasting as a means of getting things done (Isa. 58:6), and Jesus also fasted. If He did, who are you not to do so as well?

Fasting is not just doing away with food, but leaving food to be with God. It is a spiritual activity that should receive all of your concentration. Fasting not only serves your spiritual relationship with God, but it also refreshes your health. If you have ever really given yourself to fasting and prayer, you will notice the freshening that follows. You feel light and your health comes back to you with new vigor.

> *"Is not this the fast I have chosen? To loose the bands of wickedness, to undo the heavy burdens, and to let the oppressed go free, and that ye break every yoke? . . . . Then shall thy light break forth as the morning, and thine health shall spring forth speedily: and thy righteousness shall go before thee; the glory of the Lord shall be thy reward." Isaiah 58:6–8*

> *"But they that wait upon the Lord shall renew their strength; they shall mount up with wings as eagles; they shall run, and not be weary; and they shall walk, and not faint." Isaiah 40:31*

Fasting is both medically and spiritually recognized as a means of keeping your health alive. Do it, and you will enjoy the benefits.

4. CONFESSING THE SCRIPTURE

What you say is what you will have. Speak health always. Do not acknowledge sickness in your body. Declare every time, boldly, the Word of God that grants you divine health, and you will stay healthy throughout the days of your life. Having the Scriptures in your heart every day and confessing them concerning every situation of life gives you an edge over the devil, our arch enemy.

In chapter 3 of this book, I have dealt with confessing the Word of God, presenting to you the fact that you can use your mouth to either put away something or bring anything into your life, all by what you speak on daily basis.

Luke 21:15 says:

"For I will give you a mouth and wisdom, which all your adversaries shall not be able to gainsay nor resist."

This means that what you say cannot be overruled by any of your enemies, including sicknesses and diseases.

5. YOUR SERVICE IN GOD'S HOUSE

The Scriptures make it clear that your service to God will cause God to take away sickness from you.

"And ye shall serve the Lord your God, and he shall bless thy bread, and thy water; and I will take sickness away from the midst of thee." Exodus 23:25

So, make sure there is something you do for God in your church and in your community that is a service unto God, and make sure you do it will all your heart.

6. HOLINESS

Sin is one of the easiest ways to destroy your health. You cannot persist in sinful habits and expect to be in divine health.

> *"And [he] said, if thou wilt diligently hearken to the voice of the Lord thy God, and wilt do that which is right in his sight, and wilt give ear to his commandments, and keep all his statures, I will put none of these diseases upon thee, which I have brought upon the Egyptians: for I am the Lord that healeth thee." Exodus 15:26*

The above condition for you not to encounter sicknesses and diseases is to obey the commandments of your God. This simply means that you should not live in sin, because anything you do outside divine instruction presented to you, to be followed by God in your day-to-day living, is a sin.

> *"Shall we continue in sin, that grace may abound? God forbid." Romans 6:1–2*

To live in sin and expect to enjoy the grace of divine health is impossible. Grace for divine health cannot flourish in an atmosphere polluted by sin. Sin brought sicknesses, and to eradicate sickness, therefore, you

◆ *Maintaining Divine Health* ◆

must turn your back on sinning and allow holiness to prevail for divine health may stay.

I so believe that if you will put these above things in place in your life, you will surely, by His grace, experience divine health and stay healthy throughout the days of your life. May your divine healing be permanent, and may you stay healthy forever in Jesus's name. Amen.

Helpful Healing And Long-Life Scripture

"And [he] said, If thou wilt diligently hearken to the voice of the Lord thy God, and wilt do that which is right in his sight, and wilt give ear to his commandments, and keep all his statutes, I will put none of these diseases upon thee, which I have brought upon the Egyptians: for I am the Lord that healeth thee." Exodus 15:26

"And ye shall serve the Lord your God, and he shall bless thy bread, and thy water; and I will take sickness away from the midst of thee." Exodus 23:25

"And the Lord will take away from thee all sickness, and will put none of the evil diseases of Egypt, which thou knowest, upon thee; but will lay them upon all them that hate thee." Deuteronomy 7:15

"Give unto the Lord, O ye mighty, give unto the Lord glory and strength." Psalm 29:1

"The Lord will strengthen him upon the bed of languishing: thou wilt make all his bed in his sickness." Psalm 41:3

"Why art thou cast down, O my soul? and why art thou disquieted within me? hope in God: for I shall yet praise him, who is the health of my countenance, and my God." Psalm 43:5

"With long life will I satisfy him, and shew him my salvation." Psalm 91:16

"Bless the Lord, O my soul and forget not all his benefits: Who forgiveth all thine iniquities; who healeth all thy diseases." Psalm 103:2–3

"He sent his word, and healed them, and delivered them from their destructions." Psalm 107:20

"I shall not die, but live, and declare the works of the Lord." Psalm 118:17

♦ Helpful Healing And Long-life Scripture ♦

"O Lord, by these things men live, and in all these things is the life of my spirit: so wilt thou recover me, and make me to live." Isaiah 38:16

"But they that wait upon the Lord shall renew their strength; they shall mount up with wings as eagles; they shall run, and not be weary; and they shall walk, and not faint." Isaiah 40:31

"Surely he hath borne our griefs, and carried our sorrows: yet we did esteem him stricken, smitten of God, and afflicted. But he was wounded for our transgressions, he was bruised for our iniquities: the chastisement of our peace was upon him; and with his stripes we are healed." Isaiah 53:4–5

"I create the fruit of the lips; Peace, peace to him that is far off, and to him that is near, saith the Lord; and I will heal him." Isaiah 57:19

"For I will restore health unto thee, and I will heal thee of thy wounds, saith the Lord; because they called thee an Outcast, saying,

This is Zion, whom no man seeketh after."
Jeremiah 30:17

"Behold, I will bring it health and cure, and I will cure them, and will reveal unto them the abundance of peace and truth."
Jeremiah 33:6

"I will seek that which was lost, and bring again that which was driven away, and will bind up that which was broken, and will strengthen that which was sick: but I will destroy the fat and the strong; I will feed them with judgment." Ezekiel 34:16

"And Jesus went about all Galilee, teaching in their synagogues, and preaching the gospel of the kingdom, and healing all manner of sickness and all manner of disease among the people." Matthew 4:23

"That it might be fulfilled which was spoken by Esaias the prophet, saying, Himself took our infirmities, and bare our sicknesses." Matthew 8:17

"But when Jesus heard that, he said unto them, They that be whole need not a physician, but they that are sick." Matthew 9:12

♦ *Helpful Healing And Long-life Scripture* ♦

"The Spirit of the Lord is upon me, because he hath anointed me to preach the gospel to the poor; he hath sent me to heal the brokenhearted, to preach deliverance to the captives, and recovering of sight to the blind, to set at liberty them that are bruised[.]" Luk 4:18

"But if the Spirit of him that raised up Jesus from the dead dwell in you, he that raised up Christ from the dead shall also quicken your mortal bodies by his Spirit that dwelleth in you." Romans 8:11

"Who his own self bare our sins in his own body on the tree, that we, being dead to sins, should live unto righteousness: by whose stripes ye were healed. For ye were as sheep going astray; but are now returned unto the Shepherd and Bishop of your souls." 1 Peter 2:24-25

"Beloved, I wish above all things that thou mayest prosper and be in health, even as thy soul prospereth." 3 John 1:2

HELPFUL PRAYER POINTS

―――◆―――

YOU CAN PRAY FOR DIVINE HEALING BY yourself, and God will heal you. These prayer points will help you in praying for your healing and for that of others. It is "operation do it yourself."

Confess the following Scriptures out loud:

"And ye shall serve the Lord your God, and he shall bless thy bread, and thy water; and I will take sickness away from the midst of thee." Exodus 23:15

"But unto you that fear my name shall the son of righteousness arise with healing in his wings; and ye shall go forth, and grow up as calves of the stall." Malachi 4:2.

"Who his own self bare our sins in his own body on the tree, that we, being dead to sins, should live unto righteousness: by whose stripes ye were healed." 1 Peter 2:24

1. Lord, I thank you for Your divine provision for healing.
2. Lord, I thank you for Your mighty power that can heal all manner of sicknesses and diseases.
3. Lord, let Your healing hand be stretched out upon my life now, in the name of Jesus.
4. Heal me, O Lord, by Your mighty hand of healing in Jesus's name.
5. Deliver me, O Lord, by Your mighty hand of deliverance in Jesus's name.
6. I command all the organisms that are causing this sickness in my body to die in Jesus's name.
7. I command the root of this sickness and disease in my life to be destroyed in Jesus's name.
8. Lord, let Your hand of miracles heal my infirmities in the name of Jesus.
9. May every infirmity come out now with all of its roots, in the name of Jesus.
10. May every instrument of the enemy that is being used against my health be destroyed in Jesus's name.
11. I destroy every conscious and unconscious covenant with sickness and disease in the name of Jesus.
12. Holy Ghost fire, destroy the root of this sickness in my body in the name of Jesus.
13. I take authority over every agent of sickness working against my health in the name of Jesus.

◆ Helpful Prayer Points ◆

14. I command all arrows of sickness and diseases to return to the sender in the name of Jesus.
15. I receive perfect healing from heaven in the name of Jesus.
16. I command all demons of sicknesses and diseases to get out of my body in the name of Jesus.
17. Let the water and the blood in my body be transfused with the blood of Jesus.
18. May all fountains of sicknesses and diseases in my life dry up now in the name of Jesus.
19. I destroy the grip and operation of sickness in my life in the name of Jesus.
20. Heal me, O Lord, with Your healing balm in the name of Jesus.
21. May every power militating against my health be destroyed in the name of Jesus.
22. Let my body receive the strength of the Holy Ghost in the name of Jesus.
23. Let the healing anointing rest upon me now in the name of Jesus.
24. I receive my healing in Jesus's name.
25. Thank you, God, for answering my prayers.

BIBLIOGRAPHY

Hagin, Kenneth E. *The Healing Anointing*. Kenneth Hagin Ministries, Tulsa, OK, USA. (2000).

Jakes, T.D. *God Longs to Heal You*. Destiny Image Publishers Inc. Shippensburg, PA USA. (1995).

Roberts, Oral. *If You Need Healing Do These Things*. Oral Roberts Evangelistic

ALSO BY DR. DAVID A. ADEBOYE

- YOU CAN HEAR GOD TOO!
- WISDOM FOR DAILY LIVING
- FOUR KEYS TO TURNING YOUR SEASON AROUND
- 10 LESSONS ALL FATHERS MUST TEACH THEIR CHILDREN

Lightning Source UK Ltd.
Milton Keynes UK
UKHW011016050520
362811UK00001B/16